Empowered Every Day:

31 Daily Affirmations for a Positive Life

My Goal for the next 31 days is to:

____

____

____

____

____

Thoughts

I am a powerful creator of my reality.

Thoughts

I am filled with gratitude for every moment.

Thoughts

I am a positive influence on others.

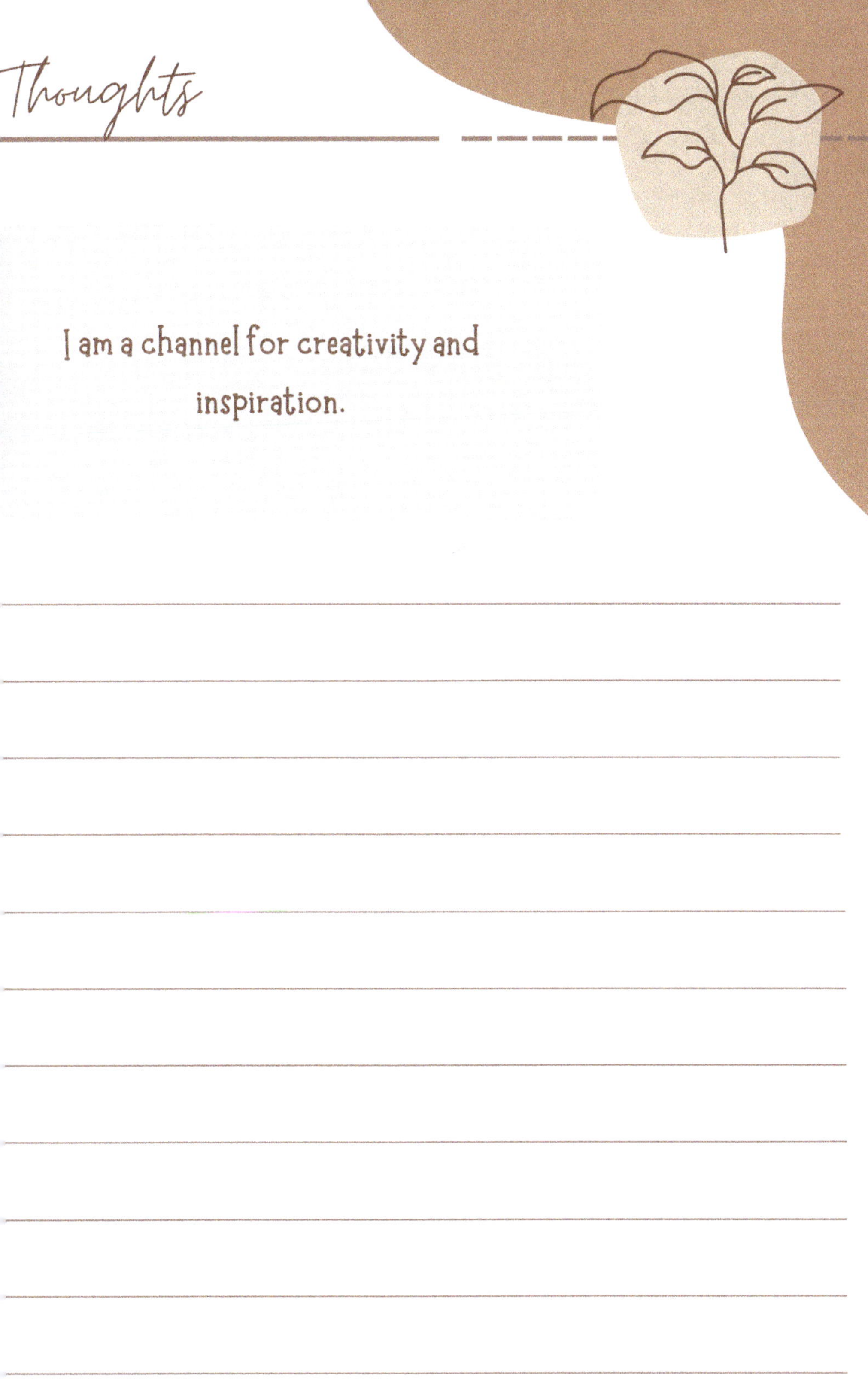

I am a channel for creativity and inspiration.

Thoughts

I am in tune with my inner wisdom.

I am open to receiving abundance
in all its forms.

Thoughts

I am a source of love and light.

Thoughts

I am aligned with my true purpose.

Thoughts

I am the author of my own story.

I am a magnet for positive people and experiences.

I am resilient, and I can overcome any obstacle.

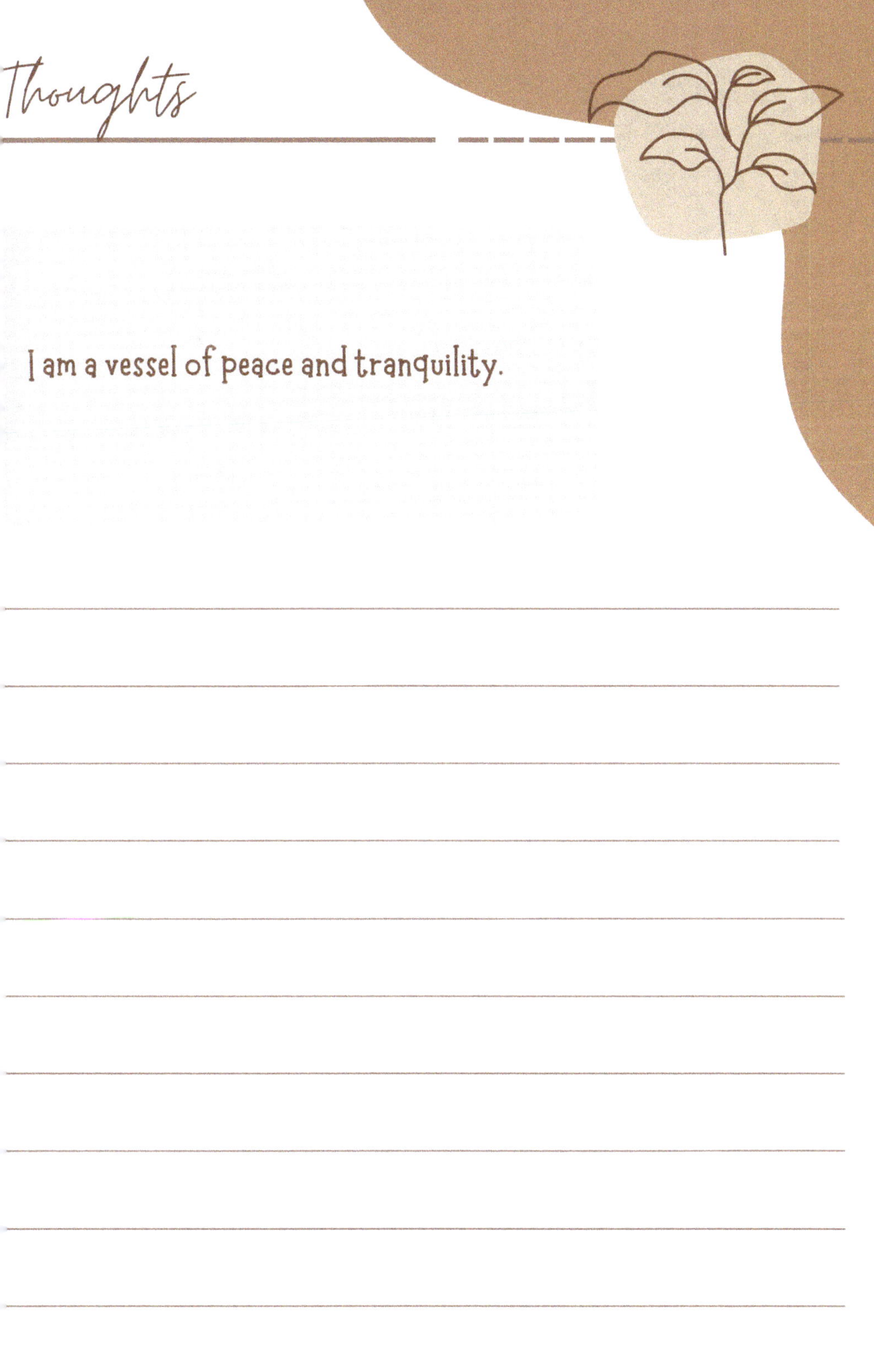

Thoughts

I am a vessel of peace and tranquility.

I am a source of strength for
myself and others.

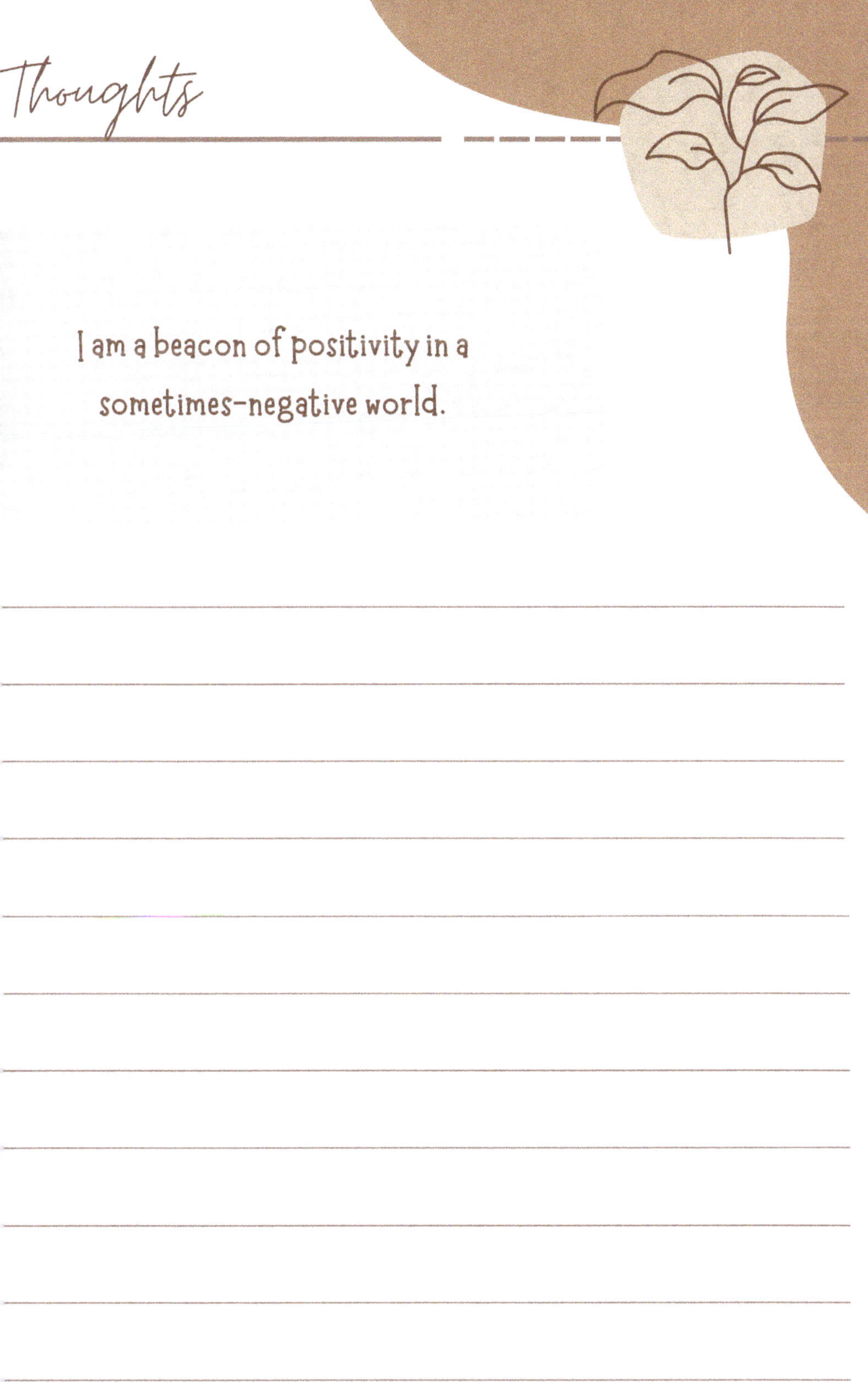

I am a beacon of positivity in a
sometimes-negative world.

I am grateful for the lesson's life teaches me.

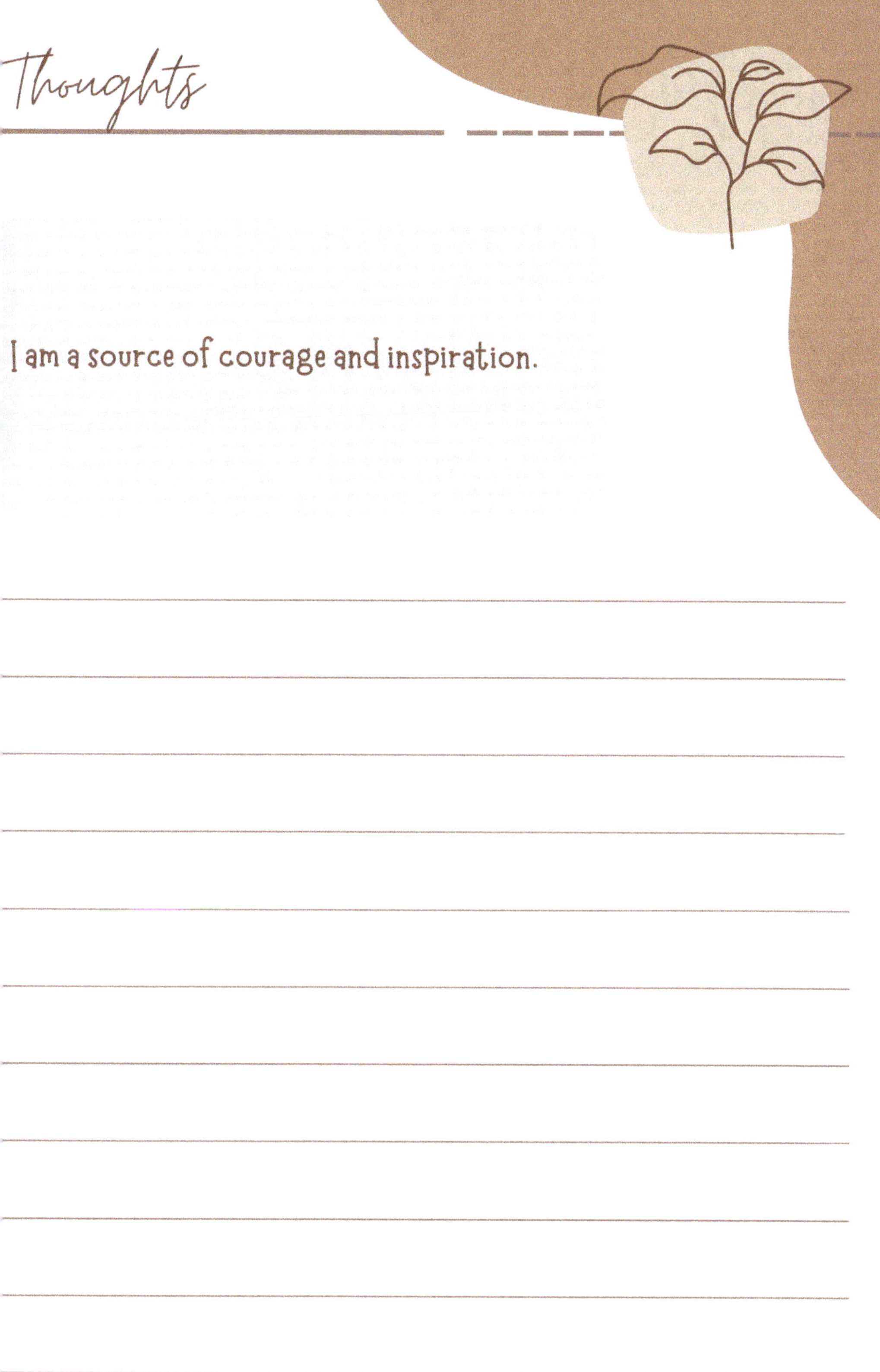

Thoughts

I am a source of courage and inspiration.

Thoughts

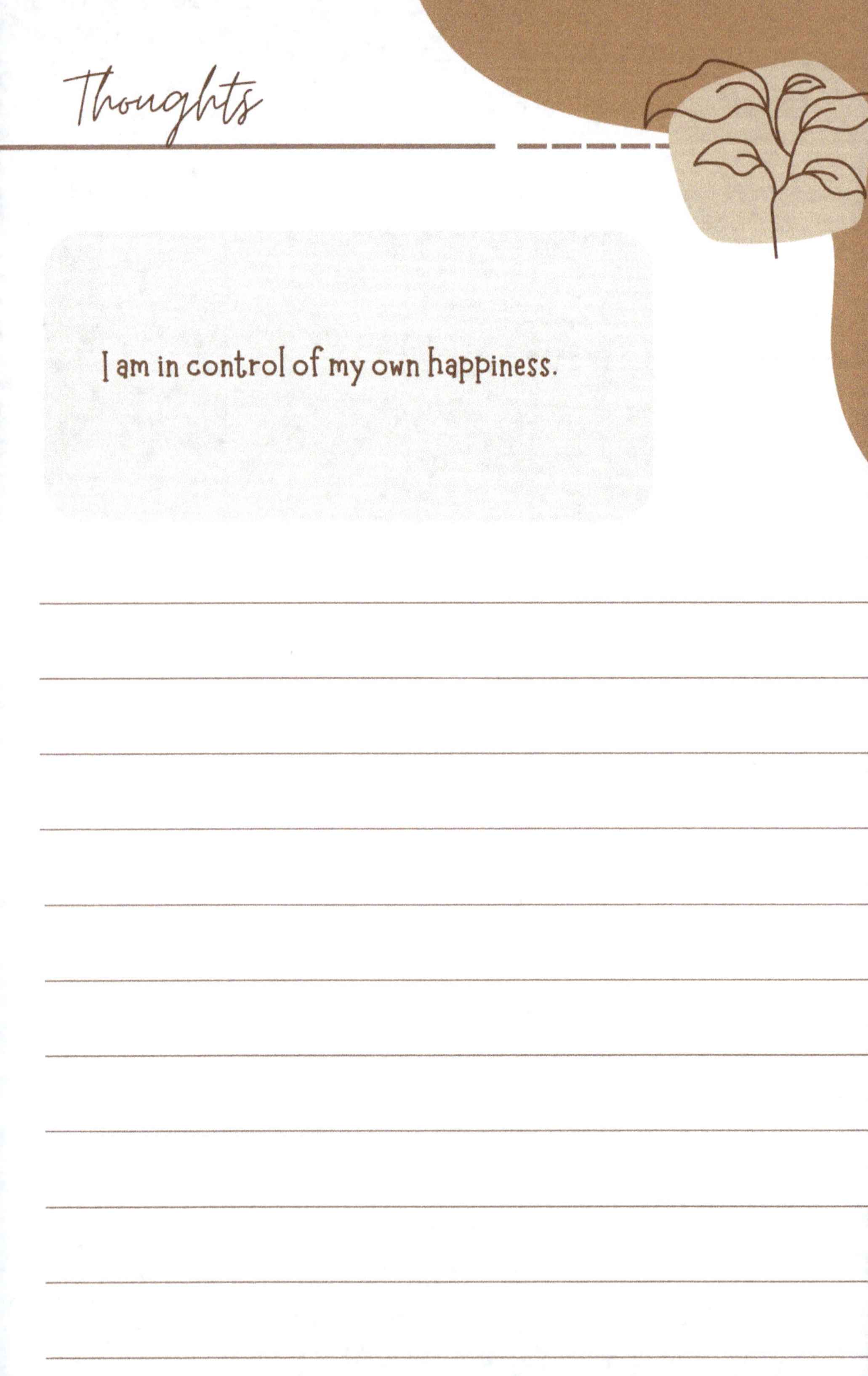

I am in control of my own happiness.

Thoughts

I am worthy of love and respect.

I am a force for change and
transformation.

I am worthy of love and acceptance.

Thoughts

I am resilient and can overcome any challenge.

Thoughts

I am surrounded by abundance.

Thoughts
I can achieve my dreams.

Thoughts

I am enough just as I am.

I am constantly growing and improving.

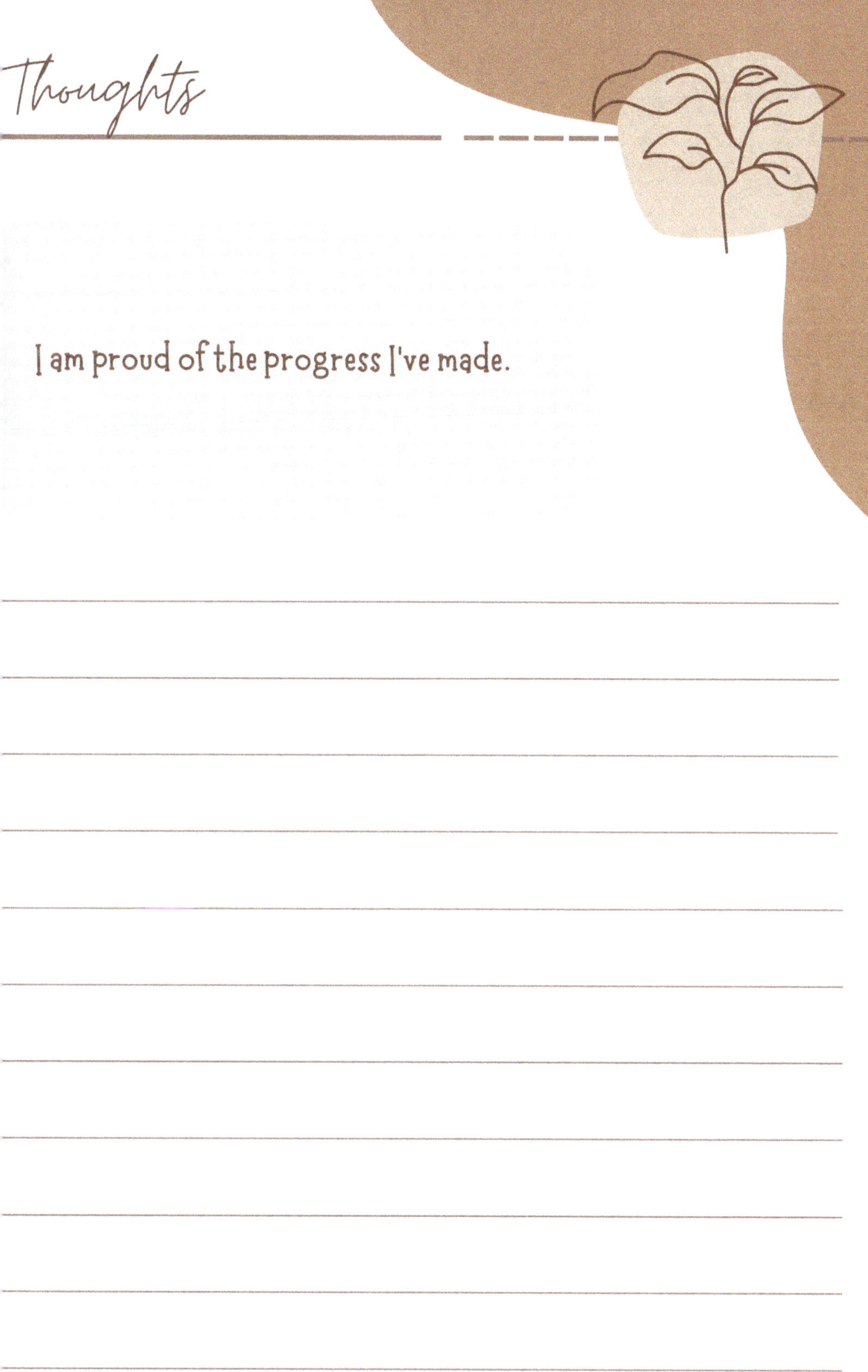

Thoughts

I am proud of the progress I've made.

I am a beacon of positivity and light.

Thoughts

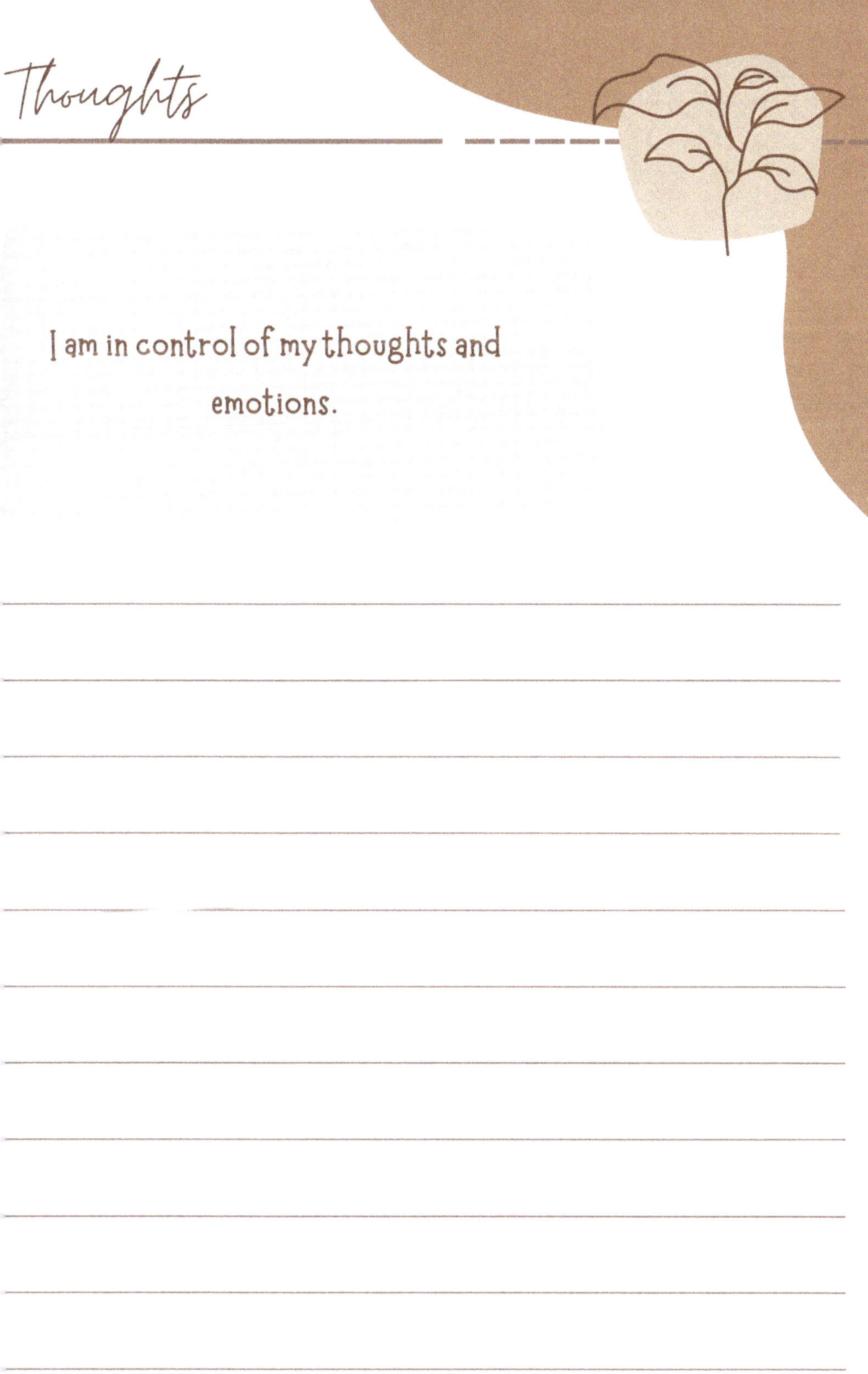

I am in control of my thoughts and
emotions.

Thoughts

I am a source of inspiration for others.

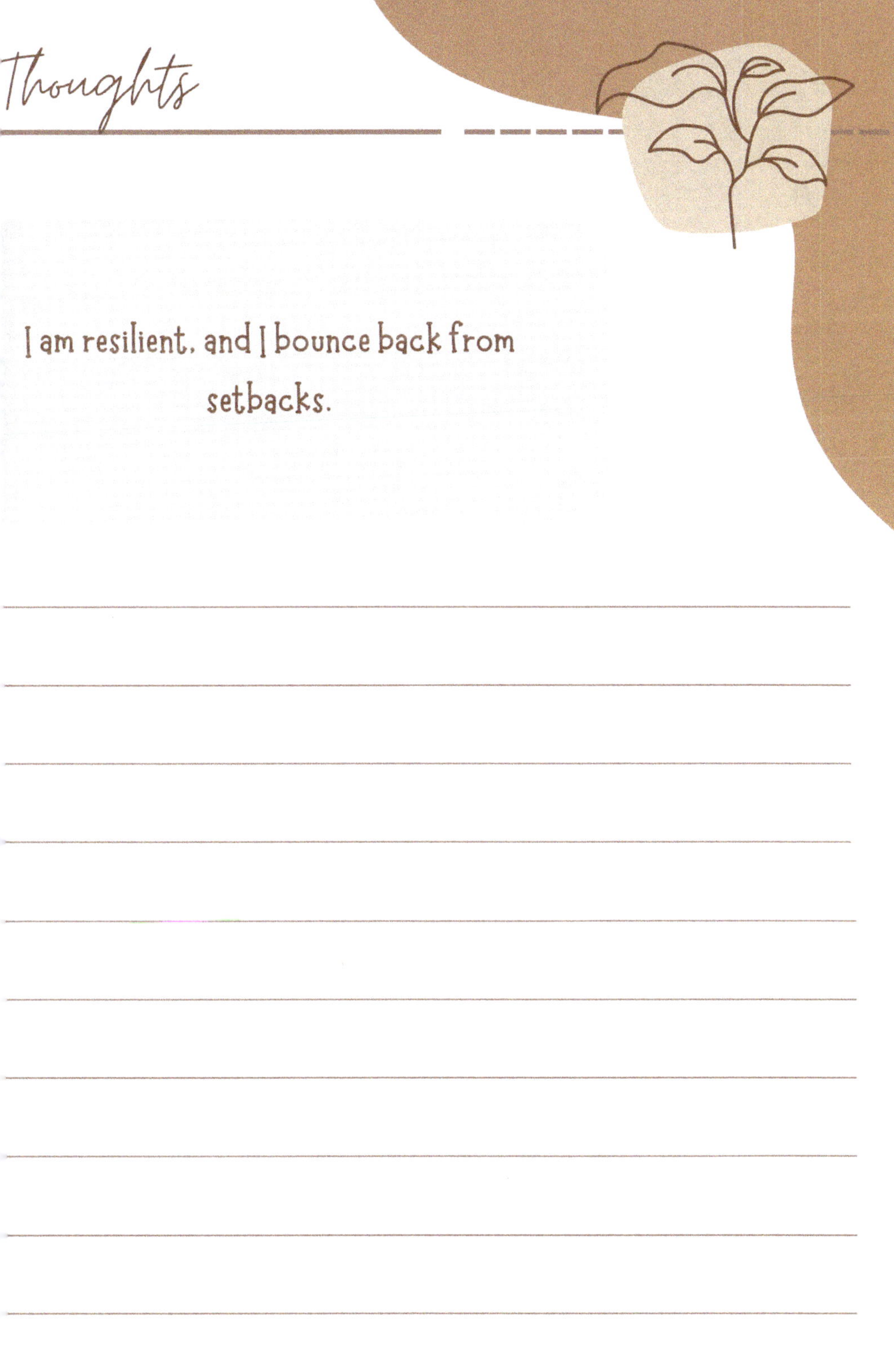

Thoughts

I am resilient, and I bounce back from setbacks.

I am a vessel of wisdom and strength.